Pittsburgh and Other Poems

Alan Ira Gordon

Pittsburgh and Other Poems
By Alan Ira Gordon

All rights reserved. No part of this book may be reproduced or transmitted in any form or by any means, electronic or mechanical, including photocopying or recording or by any information storage and retrieval systems, without expressed written consent of the author and/or artists.

Pittsburgh and Other Poems is a work of fiction. Names, characters, places, and incidents are products of the author's imagination. Any resemblance to actual events or persons, living or dead, is entirely coincidental.

Poem copyrights owned by Alan Ira Gordon
Cover illustration "Pittsburgh"
Cover design by Marcia A. Borell

First Printing
June 2024

Hiraeth Publishing
P.O. Box 1248
Tularosa, NM 88352
e-mail: hiraethsubs@yahoo.com

Visit www.hiraethsffh.com for online science fiction, fantasy, horror, scifaiku, and more. Stop by our online bookstore for novels, magazines, anthologies, and collections. Support the small, independent press and your First Amendment rights.

For Elizabeth and Joey

For Priscilla

For Gary and Susie

For Paul Szlosek

Also by Alan Ira Gordon

Planet Hunter

The Doggo Book

Tales From the Quantum Café

(All titles available from Hiraeth Publishing)

Introduction

At first glance, it may seem that the selected poems in this collection are connected simply by being an assemblage of science fiction, fantasy and horror poems. And that's certainly true.

But that's not the only connectivity between these poems. In my day job I'm an urban planner, having previously worked in various communities and now serving as an Urban Planning Instructor in the Urban Studies Department at Worcester State University. And one thing that I've learned from the discipline of urbanism is how central the importance of a sense of place is to people.

Sometimes a sense of place is easy to identify and understand. In those instances, it can be a physical city, town, neighborhood or just a piece of property. Other times it can be a point in time, either past, present or future. And in yet other instances it can be a more exotic or alien sense of place, perhaps intergalactic, or multi-universe, even an alternate reality version of a well-known place and time, existing at a quantum point or merely within the minds of writers and readers.

I believe that connecting our real-world with the fantastic can be both an effective and entertaining role of genre poetry. And that's why I selected as the lead poem in this collection "Pittsburgh Temporal Transfer Station," thus lending that particular poem's sense of place to this book's title. Both within our general culture and the urban planning discipline, the City of Pittsburgh is historically known as a "rustbelt city," evolving as an historically industrial American urban center, then falling on hard times as the economy, culture and the world in general changed.

But then an amazing thing happened: in the latter years of the 20th century, Pittsburgh re-invented itself, in many ways too numerous to describe in this Introduction, but the result being a 21st century model of transformation. Earlier generations of Americans wouldn't recognize today's elements of Pittsburgh (as well as other modern-day cities), seeing such changes as a science fiction and/or fantasy reality. Hence the idea for the lead poem, that of a futuristic time-travel center located within the renovated building of a previous Pittsburgh historic train station.

In echoing that sense, I think that all of the poems in this book embody that concept, exploring in poetic form various ideas of sense of place, whether physical locations, points in time or ideas of place that could only exist (for now, at least) within the creative realms of science fiction, fantasy and/or horror. So I hope that readers enjoy their trips to the various explored places within these poems.

Before you move on from this Introduction, a few thanks are in order. My sincere thank you to the following editors and mentors who have been kind enough to advise, edit /or publish my genre poetry in various magazines and collections: F. J. Bergmann, Bruce Boston, Jean-Paul Garnier, Vince Goleta, Emily Hockaday, and Marge Simon. (Marge, I'd list you first but I went alphabetical!). And last but believe me hardly least, actually most of all, Tyree Campbell, for whom I am so grateful and have so many ways of describing: publisher, editor, mentor, good solid friend and most importantly, fellow doggo/husky person! Thank you all for being there for and with me along my poetry writing path.

Alan Ira Gordon
Worcester, Massachusetts
October 2023

Table Of Contents

Pittsburgh Temporal Transfer Station
Quantum Mechanics & Auto Body Repair
In Memory Yet Green

15   To The Stars

When My Mother Walked on Titan
Spacely Space Sprockets Wants You!
Social Distancing Implemented
Chuck Berry At The End Of Time
Feng Shui
Robert Goddard At Roswell
From Whence The Songbird Sings
A Day In The Life
Dating The Borg (Or How I Tried To Love A Hive Mentality)
The Maestro's Final Work
These Are Not The Droids You're Looking For

31   Fantastic Beasts and Such

Pinocchio Plays The Cotton Club
Incident At Midnight: Massachusetts Turnpike Exit #2
Monster Mash
Werewolf Doggy Bag

37   Vampire Triptych

Vampire Selfies
Because The Night
Untitled Vampire Poem

Pocket Universe #8: Lucy, The Monster Hunter
Pocket Universe #18: Chicago Queenpin
Apocalyptica
Alien Bachelorette Party
Shake Your Robot!
Second Chances
Clash Of Paradigms
Schrodinger's Groceries
Schrodinger's Wallet Effect
When Your Body Fails You

53   **Music**

Robert Johnson, Mississippi Delta Crossroads (1936)
Pocket Universe #83: Ozzy Boards
The Crazy Train
Pocket Universe #611: Ladies & Gentlemen, The Beatles!
She Loves You, Yeah, Yeah, Yeah...
The Intergalactic Dogma Of The Lizard King
Time-Traveling T.V. Weatherman
Illogic Is Our Freedom
Unfortunate Singularity
I've Seen The Ruby Slippers

Pittsburgh Temporal Transfer Station

Main Concourse, 11:17 a.m., June 15, 2097

From the other side
of the surging time-traveling crowd
I see her with three other Girl
Scouts manning their cookie table.

I hobble over and lean on my cane
as our eyes meet and instinctively
she knows we're one (same as I
recall before on this day).

"I like your sparkly cane," she says.
"I know," I reply. "That's why
I finally bought it just last year."
And we both laugh.

I purchase a box of Samoas,
open it and chew on one slowly;
we just look at each other, our
eyes saying all that need to be said.

I turn as if to go but don't leave
just yet, waiting...waiting...
waiting...from this side and time
I know it's coming.

"Hey...me," she says softly.
I slowly pivot and face her,
eyes re-locking. "Tell me," she
continues. "Did we do great things?"

I answer with a short barking
laugh, so integral to our being
that she has her clear answer.

And with unanticipated renewal
I march off to catch my time train.

(2023 Rhysling Award Nominee Finalist)

Quantum Mechanics & Auto Body Repair

Before the Sweet Ride's hood is popped,
the engine cylinders are both running
smoothly and mis-firing.

Before the hydraulic lift rises,
the undercarriage is both pristine
and cracked with leaking oil.

Before the tires are removed, the brake
pads are both newly thick and worn-thin
begging for a pad-and-rotor-change.

And before you unfold the invoice,
the bill is both a credit card max-out
and a dodge-the-bullet lowly token fee.

It doesn't matter if you drive by following
careful road rules or alternatively kick-
the-carbon out in a tire-squealing road rage.

Both simultaneously waves and particles,
it's out of your hands and up to the immutable
laws and boundaries of the functioning universe.

So don't think about it. Just drive the damn car.
And let the physics of the repair shop
play it all out.

In Memory Yet Green

*I'll bring you a present from
Earth when I come to you,*
she messaged. *Anything you want.
Just name it.*

I've lived on this dust-
choked planet for so very long,
that what I desire the most
has evolved from the physical
to that more fleeting, cradled
only in my mind's memory of
what once was and doesn't
exist here.

I want to be honest and message
her back: *The smell of rain.
Can you bring it for me?
I can't remember it anymore.
And I need to.*

My hands hesitate over the message
board. I can't ask, for how could she
really bring it here to this
dry and dusty place?
So I send instead: *Only you.
You're all I need.*
And I realize that it's true.
When she arrives, I'll hold her
and remember all.

Of Earth.
Of Home.
Of Her.
And I'll smell the rain again.

(2021 Rhysling Award Nominee)

To The Stars

When My Mother Walked On Titan

When she was Commander of The First
Exploration Party, I asked her to bring
me back something unique to the history
of the event: perhaps a piece of the moon
or maybe a bit of any new life
discovered.

Now decades later, on occasions that warrant
a needed dose of levity, I unwrap again
her gift and proudly wear it to the delight
of all, who enjoy the well-worn words
across the front of my Titan Expedition
gift:

> *My Mom Went To Titan*
> *And All She Brought Me Back*
> *Was This Lousy T-Shirt*

Spacely Space Sprockets Wants You!

We're not a union shop,
that's fer certain
and we're constantly pushin' the envelope;
no "180 Days Without an Industrial
Accident" fer us.

No, folks get offed round here,
sometimes it seems on an hourly
basis. Ya can get fried in a particle
accelerator, maybe messed-up in a
quantum drive.

And believe me, if yer unlucky
enough ta trip into the R&D Division's
demo teleportation device,
ya sure-as-sure won't be yerself
on the other side.
If ya know what I mean.

But at the end
of the long, long work day?
Even if yer hands are cut ta ribbons
or yer foamin' at the mouth?
It's still. Still. All worth it.

'Cause we're buildin' spaceships.
Ta the stars.

Social distancing implemented:
intergalactic pandemic lasts so long,
we forgot where we placed
that blue-green world
with the young, bickering race.

Chuck Berry At The End Of Time

As Voyager I is finally intercepted
its recorded message is decrypted
by alien retrievers and The Sagan Greeting
bullets to the top of the interstellar
entertainment charts. Who knew
that universal sensibilities would find
humanity's greeting montage as the most
hysterically funny audio of all space
and time?

Feng Shui

1. Place nine planets in an elliptical orbit about a Class G star;

2. When seeding for life, commence at the third orbital outward for the the most harmonious planting;

3. *Bagua* will derive from eight clockwise orbits. You may include one additional counter-clockwise path;

4. Sprinkle your moons at random both in size and location for a most auspicious result;

5. Be minimal regarding the inclusion of rings and gas giants.

A traveling along this five-step path will manifest in a good system *Qi*.

Robert Goddard At Roswell

Back home in Worcester, Massachusetts
no matter how hard he tries
the breakthrough eludes him,
as rocket-after-rocket
crashes and burns
in Aunt Effie's cabbage field.

So a phone call is made
for careful conversation
and a relocation is arranged
to Roswell in New Mexico.

The little green guys
of Area 51, when they meet
they like him, they do
with his shiny bald head
pencil-thin mustache
and "cahn't get they'ah from hey'ah"
New England affability.

Thus a deal is struck
shrewd as they are,
a taste of tech for a swap
of freedom.
And soon his rockets
in the hot Southwestern sky
they don't crash and burn,
but blaze straight toward the sun.

And that swap of freedom?
Begins in the form
of a baby blue '33 Nash.
Spinning wheelies round their battered ship,
they whistle and clap
as if already sprung unto the heavens

"We'll see you on the moon, Big Bob!
Yes, we will! E-I-E-I-Oh!"

As they honk and giggle through
the rising desert dust,
he pauses, wrench in hand
and wiping sweat from brow
with a formal country boy smile
nods quietly in acknowledgement
and sincere thanks.

Then turns back toward his task
to relaunch them to the stars.

(2020 Rhysling Award Nominee)

From Whence The Songbird Sings

She told me one dark evening, how
on her native world she stood
waist-deep in a ruby river while
lightning chirped across an orange sky.
I fought back tears that sprang
to life from the look on her
face as she longed for home.

But in the glare of next morning's
light, I recall the cost of her
license from the import shop, and
calculate in my head the expense of
travel back to that world. Tamping
the night's memory deep down and back
inside, I begin the day as always
by unlocking her gilded cage.

A Day In The Life

I know what
your starship Earthling crewmates
call my people:
Mayflies.

It's a nice-sounding word
in our respective tongues
but I know it's an insult
uttered in mocking condescension.

Your people pity and look down
on us, as we're the only known
sentient species with the lifespan
of a single day.

But know this: you humans
have a saying, I can't recall it
exactly, but the point being
that a life lived brightest, of even
the shortest length is one
most worth living.

And nature has given my people
a unique talent, compensation
as it were: our ultra-fast ability
to gauge situations and people within
our hyper-accentuated timespan.

So I can say to you with complete
certainty: you, yourself are different
from your starship Earthling crewmates.
For you truly empathize with and respect us,
indeed, you may even love us.
And we appreciate that, very much.

As for me, personally? I can say
with all complete sincerity that it's been
a genuine pleasure getting to know
you so well.

In these last few moments
of my life.

Dating The Borg (Or How I Tried To Love A Hive Mentality)

It wasn't meant to be
for many reasons, the first sign
being that He/She/They would send
a different member of The Collective to
each of our dates. It was all the same
to them. But not to me.

I could go on-and-on, but getting
to the point, the final straw being that
you know His/Her/Their well-known
catchphrase: *We are The Borg, resistance
is futile*? One day I realized that
He/She/They never, ever even once
used it on me.

That's when I realized that His/Her/Their hearts
just weren't in it, were just going through
the motions. So I did us all a favor and
pulled the relationship plug myself.
I could feel the relief just ripple
through The Collective.

It's all water under the bridge, now. We're
past it o.k. and actually on good terms. And come
each holiday season, He/She/They still takes
a moment to stop and send me a Christmas
card from whatever sector of the universe
that He/She/They are busy assimilating.

The Maestro's Final Work

After he moved on from this reality's plane,
The Institute held a lottery among his students
(as was the tradition), I being fortunate of
the selected honor to complete
his final workpiece.

He left it just about complete, really,
needing only a superficial touch-up
or two. The Maestro wasn't sensitive
of such touches, often indulging his students'
offered critiques to lightly add elements
that he himself had not included, as
offered-up with respect and sincerity.

I wished to honor his legacy of
generosity as our Teacher, Mentor and Sage.
Thus, I lightly incorporated three gentlest
of light brushstrokes to this, the mosaic
of His Final Work:

First, I modified the color of the endless
drifting sandscapes dusting the surface
of the fourth orbiting planet from the Maestro's
draft tone of a benign blue shade to instead
a final version of melancholy blood-red.

Next, I turned my attention to the sixth-
position gas giant; having been rendered
with even bands of yellow, ochre and
white under the Maestro's loving hand, I
enhanced the effect by gently braiding
about its midriff a series of rubble-strewn
orbital rings.

And finally, I lightly-sprinkled upon
the shining waters of the third orbital
the basic seeds for emerging life. Knowing
that the Maestro would have appreciated this,
the starkest simplicity of a sole planet infused
with life's potential to spread (or not) upon
its infant surface and possibly expand
onto the remaining orbitals of this smallish
solar system.

His final masterpiece, as set
gently amongst the Maestro's
panoply of stars.

These Are Not The Droids You're Looking For

I think they're adorable, but I'm a solitary voice in the wilderness; my people consider the Earth-race to be a miserable lot, a petty/bickering/fractious bunch, who if they ever get their act together would pose at the least a major annoyance to the rest of the universe.

But it's the upper-level Artificial Intelligence races that pose the real threat to the Earthlings. That bunch are on the constant Galactic Prowl to cull-out youngling organic species. Those who hold the potential for evolving into a legitimate counter to their goal of AI galactic dominance.

And they'd heard rumors of the Earthling's toxicity, which they see in some organics as seed to bloom against them. So as the AI's began to root around for a thread to follow, a lead as it were to the Earthling's location, I made my move.

I refined my millennia's worth of coding experience into an elegant program. One that when encountered by AI consciousness would gently divert their probing discretely away from any true Earth system encounter.

I'm satisfied with its functionality so far; it's been a few centuries now and the AI's have yet to stumble across the smallish Sol System where the Earthlings dwell.

Oh, they've come close a few times. Very close,
in fact. But whenever they've tripped the wire,
my program reacts and mirages the humans.
And I can't resist a bit of humor. Like I said,
I think they're adorable, with their quaint
cinematic efforts to describe the universe.

So I took a quote from one of their outer space
films and inserted it as a line of trigger coding
for diversion: a space warrior veteran warning-
off the movie baddies. Falsifying that the film's
artificials they've come across aren't the ones
they seek to destroy. An ironic role reversal
of this real-time intergalactic blood-hunt.

But this isn't a game or a joke but rather a true
necessity. For my people don't have the personality
to confront the AI's steadily growing aggression.
Thus we're going to need younglings like
the Earther's to grow in their hidden safe havens.

Until the day when they've matured to be revealed
onto the galactic stage and take-on the AI's.
And hopefully save us all.
From the true Evil Empire.

Fantastic Beasts and Such

Pinocchio Plays The Cotton Club

So how can I be real, Pops?
he asks the puppet maker.
Joe Petto exhales a long reefer
stream while reaching under
his workbench for the velvet-lined
case. Removing the gleaming brass
trumpet, he flexes the valves
and places the instrument
between the dark mahogany
fingers of his carved-son.

It won't come soon and it won't
be easy, he tells the wooden lad.
But with time and effort,
and hard work mixed-in
with a splinter or two,
you can reach the real, taste
it and maybe even become it.

13 Years Later:
After 2:00 A.M. only the diehards
are still in the club;
onstage he's fronting his back-up
of broken toy jazzy dreamers.
He leads them through some
Coltrane, then lifts into Miles Davis
followed-by a run of Marsalis.

Without warning, he drops the room
into uncharted waters with
his own piece: as his solo
climbs higher and higher, even
the club's smoke stands still
to watch and appreciate and begin
to fall in love.

He's not there yet, not completely,
but getting oh so closer, near
enough to feel it rising in
his darkwood fingers, hear it
in his ears and sense it in his soul.
He's confident now that he'll taste
it and become one with it, still
as wooden a figure as the day
he was built, but now just as real as
the journey and the moment
and the sound.

For my father Malcolm Gordon

(2019 Rhysling Award Nominee)

Incident At Midnight: Massachusetts Turnpike Exit #2

Working the tollbooth night shift
at the deep Berkshire Pike access
this side of Great Barrington,
we're trained to take a deep breath
at a minute-to-midnight
close our eyes and wait a bit,
ignoring the spectral screams
as whatever apparates from
the bewitched Puritan hills
traverses our turnstiles.

Some say the Massachusetts Turnpike
Authority dropped the tolls
on an ancient Indian burial ground,
while others claim it's the souls
of restless Colonial forebears
eternally bickering over land titles,
township liens and the like.

And each New England summertime
at least one seasonal tollbooth intern,
some stubborn college kid out of Boston
opens his or her eyes during
the nightly ritual.

The Town ambulance efficiently whisks
them away, swaddled-in
straight-jacket secureness,
their babbling in accompaniment
to the ghostling traveler's call.

Monster Mash

Checking under the bed
and in the deep, dark
closet, as well as in all
of the dresser drawers.

Assuring my hell-spawn that
there are no scary humans lurking
about to jump-out and terrify
with their insidious talk about
hedge fund investments,
car care maintenance or slides
of what they did on their
summer vacation.

werewolf doggy bag
to finish the human entrée
re-heated tomorrow evening

Vampire Triptych

Vampire Selfies

None of the Counts
appear in the photos,
of course.
But the scenic backgrounds
are so beautiful.

(2022 SFPA Dwarf Star Award Nominee)

Because The Night

Climate change-induced mega
forest fires raging Earth-wide,
transforming nighttime into endless
daylight:

Vampires are the first
to go extinct.

Latest teen vampire craze:
Baby-stepping into the edge of daylight.
Kids these days have no sense
of their own mortality.

Pocket Universe #8: Lucy, The Monster Hunter

"Row faster, you blockhead!"
she shouts into the rising wind.
Charlie puts his back into it
really pressing the oars
ignoring the canvas-covered lump
at his feet
as the rowboat bobs atop the choppy sea.

Why do I let her boss me around?
he asks himself
*First, the thing with the football
and now this.
She's right...I am a blockhead.*

His thoughts are interrupted
as they reach the spot.
Lucy stands in the prow
and glares at Charlie
with a menacing look.
"All right, Brown, give me a hand."

Together, they wrestle the canvas
off of the prostate figure
curled fetal-like at their feet.
"Shouldn't we wake him?" Charlie asks.
"The drug'll wear-off fine," Lucy snarls.
"Soon as he hits the water."

And with a one and a two
and then a three
they toss him overboard.

He instantly awakens
spluttering and splashing about
the raw and battering waves.
"Lucy, for God's sake! Help me!"

She shouts over the howling wind.
"Help you? No, little brother,
for once, you're going to help *me*!"
Lucy retrieves an object
from the rowboat floor and tosses it
at the bobbing boy.
"Here's hoping your damn blanket
will finally do you some good!"

Just then the sea begins to boil
near the boy, and before not long
The Kraken arises from the depths
bellowing in pure might.
As the boys scream
Lucy shouts triumphantly
"That's right, you stupid bastard!
Take the bloody bait!"

Charlie points and shouts
"Lucy, it's heading for Linus!
Do something!"
Her eyes blazing with bloodlust
she shouts over the monstrous bellow:
"Oh, I'll do something, all right!
I'll kill the monster that killed
my parents!" She turns toward Charlie
as The Kraken swiftly feasts
on the floating boy.

"Now hand me that motorized harpoon
and be damned quick about it!
It'll get sleepy real fast, now
as it digests the brat and his blanket!"

Charlie hesitates for a heartbeat
then thin resolve crumbles
like a swiftly fading wave.
And with a shake of his very round head
he passes the electric harpoon
to The Madwoman Of The Seas.

Pocket Universe #18: Chicago Queenpin

She rampaged her way
up the mobster ladder,
a 1920's lioness on the midnight hunt
spewing leaden kisses
on Saint Valentine's Day,
a bloody North Side killing field.

All bowed before her criminal
syndicate, like scared little boys
at their first dance: from hizzoner
the Mayor to Ness and that weakling Nitti,
she just laughed long and aloud
entertaining the press and the Common
Folk alike, who loved her for
her brash, beauty and brains,
their hometown glamour bad girl.

Out on the Town, her ill-gained booty
on full display: "Diamonds are
a girl's best friend"
she proclaimed, a quote instantly
infamous and stolen by
Mae and Marilyn alike,
which was fine by her-honor
among thieves, you know, albeit from
the streets or Hollywood.

The end didn't come via
a tommy-gunned bang
or a pathetic declined whisper,
instead she slipped through
the nooses of rival's ordered hits
and Fed RICO hearings,
partying long and easy in

the later decades, through
Havana, Vegas and L.A., but always
the South Side Girl, her bloodied
claws still deep in the
hometown rackets. Then expiring
in her downtown penthouse bed
under a haze of Vicodin, booze
and aged notoriety.

A year later and live from
the Lexington Hotel, Geraldo
holds a nation breathless
as the doorway to her secretive
vault opens, revealing its bursting
glittering hoard and affirming
that Alyssa Capone got it right
the first time all those years
ago: in the end, diamonds are indeed
a girl's best friend.

Apocalyptica

Climate change warnings ignored,
destructive practices persist until
quicker than anyone projected
civilization and world population
freefalls into collapse, making way
for the unanticipated rise
of mammals.

Alien Bachelorette Party

After the ammonia shots are consumed and the Bride's ex-lovers are torn limb-from-limb, the partygoers conduct selection from amongst one-of-their-own a Bridesmaid, who will have the Honor of decapitating the Groom upon completion of the inevitable impregnation down the line.

Shake Your Robot!

Season #981 of *Dancing
With The Stars*
comes down to two finalists:
Unit (call me Uni, guys!) 233
versus a vintage late-21st century
Animatronic-L "Ellie" Model,
each accompanied by the requisite
Network dancing partner drone.

Five hours into The Shake-Off
it looks like Uni 233 will
close it out, after a near-perfect
algorithmically-plotted Lambata routine.

But riding a simply breathtaking
binary-modulated spurt,
Animatronic Ellie spins her drone through
a deft Tango-pairing,
seizing the day as well as
the hard-drives of the studio audience,
which erupts into a frenzy of
robotic cheers and shouts.

"I still got it," beams Animatronic Ellie,
hefting the prized winner's trophy
as she maneuvers off-stage
past studio drones wet-vacuuming
the departed audience's
oil-puddled tears of joy.

Second Chances

With time-travel so commonplace,
the IOC updates its rules and
joining both the Olympics and Paralympics on
the quadrennial schedule is the Time-Traveler's
Olympic Games (TTOC), where invited historic
athletes receive a do-over or just another
chance to thrill the crowd.

Thus Caitlyn Jenner returns to conquer
anew the decathlon, this time
on the women's side; Tommie Smith
and John Carlos repeat their '68
200-meter medals sweep as well as
their iconic Black Power/Human
Rights salute; and the penultimate wrong
is finally righted as Jim Thorpe re-smashes
the pentathlon record and rightfully
regains his stolen title, the Twenty-Third
Century stadium crowd chants of
Wa-Tho-Huk! Wa-Tho-Huk! bringing
tears to his eyes.

Clash Of Paradigms

God does not play dice
with the universe,
grumbled Einstein.

You know, you just might
be right,
replied Bohr.

Then with a Danish grin
he added:
On the other hand,
let us discuss
God's poker game.

Schrodinger's Groceries

Paper or plastic...plastic or
paper? Until the groceries are actually
bagged, they are in both.
Or none.

He contemplates and calculates on
his smart phone as the cashier
awaits his choice, while behind him
the check-out line lengthens
with impatience.

Schrodinger's Wallet Effect

Lost:

One well-worn (and favorite) men's wallet
beyond the black hole Schwarzschild Radius.

If Found:

Please notify immediately:
while of course not recoverable,
at least I'll have the satisfaction
of knowing absolutely where it is.

When Your Body Fails You

When your body fails you
and your at-birth defect consists
of having ten fingers and ten toes;

When your body fails you
and you can't breathe fresh-air methane,
forced to subsist on manufactured oxygen;

When your body fails you, your pancreas
inexplicably producing insulin of all things,
which needs to be extracted from
your system twice daily;

When your body fails you in so many
antennae-less, claw-less, horn-less,
telepathy-lacking, tentacle-missing, flight-less
teleport-less, timestream jumping-less, etc., etc.
ways;

When your body fails you, in these oh-
so-many mannerisms and directions, you must
come to terms and accept. That you're merely
human.

Things could be worse. I personally
don't know how. But I feel it and know
it. You could do worse than being
just human.

Music

Robert Johnson, Mississippi Delta Crossroads (1936)

Robert Leroy Johnson (1911-1938) is recognized as the father of American Delta Blues. He participated in only two recording sessions in 1936 and 1937 that produced 29 distinct songs.

Eric Clapton has called Johnson the most important blues singer that ever lived. Bob Dylan, Keith Richards and Robert Plant have cited Johnson's musicianship as a key influence on their own work.

Johnson's poorly documented life and death have given rise to the legend that he sold his soul to the devil at a local crossroads to achieve musical success.

~ Wikipedia

'Round midnight out at the rural crossroads,
the trail of myth and rumor ends with
an alien close encounter. They listen
to his request, then introduce him
to their spaceship's Doctor.

A simple procedure and the technology
chip is implanted in his brain. Then
Johnson's fingers move like never before
across his guitar's neck. *How can I ever
thank you?* He asks his savior from the stars.

"By answering one question," the Space Doctor
replies. *Anything for you, Doc.* The Doctor
waves a tentacled hand in accompaniment
to question.

"I told you that this is a trade-off. While enhancing your musical talent, it will severely impede your health. You will burn bright but short. And will soon die. So why agree? Why did you still have me implant your upgrade?"

*How could I not agree? Without it, I ain't much of a talent. But with it...*Johnson strums a brief tune, his fingers an enhanced blur. Then stops and gazes into the alien face. *Guess you just wouldn't understand.*

"Ah," the Doctor states. "Because I'm not human, I suppose."

No, Doc, Johnson softly replies. *Because you ain't a musician.*

They gaze at each other as the alien breaks into laughter, an unearthly sound the likes of which Johnson has never heard before. Johnson begins to play off of it, matching it with his guitar work, drawing from it a born-anew bluesy rhythm.

Huh. He stops. *Maybe I was wrong, Doc. Maybe you got the music in you, after all.*

He rises to go. "One more thing," the alien states. Johnson waits.

"When you tell this tale. As you will. For the change in you is too abrupt not to be questioned by your people,

too great. Adjust it. Just so. Tell of
this crossroads encounter. But your people
will not believe of your meeting with
us. From the stars."

Johnson thinks a moment. Then his face
breaks into a broad grin. *I got just the thing
to tell'em, Doc. They may not believe I got
my new talent by way of an unknown visitor
from above. But they'll believe that I made
a deal with a familiar figure from down
below, for sure.*

As the spaceship's door hushes open,
he slings his guitar over his back, waves
a farewell and walks out of the vessel
into the glaring heat of the Mississippi
Delta day.

Then treks northward, picking-up speed
as he heads home. For his remaining days
are so very few.

And there's so much music to be made.

Pocket Universe #83: Ozzy Boards The Crazy Train

After total achievement in his classical
music world: the symphonies, string quartets
and even the occasional operetta.

It's time for a sea change, John Osbourne
decides. Encouraged by all, he deep-dives
to the roots of his musically unrecognizable
college days (no one today would believe
who he was then).

So he tries it back on and the musical suit
still fits. Then hunkers-down and writes,
re-writing again and again until emerging
from his chrysalis, a freshling heavy metal
Prince of Darkness, having shed the caterpillar
skin of John Michael in favor of the bleeding-
red midnight butterfly of Ozzy.

Concert bookings are set and he boards
this new crazy train, ready to ride it
off the rails, if need be. And who knows,
if this Black Sabbath of a life works-out,
he might even indulge in the darkling fantasy
that he didn't dare back in his campus days.

If I do, I'll start slow, Ozzy decides.
Biting-off the head of a rubber bat
would be best for all.

Especially for the live ones.

Pocket Universe #611: Ladies & Gentlemen, The Beatles!

They were the biggest
band in the history of rock 'n roll:
Johanna, Paulina, Georgette
and Mitzy.
Ultimate rock-goddess trailblazers,
without them
there would have been
no Go-Go's, Bangles,
Bananarama or the like.

"We're more popular than God!"
Johanna crowed at their peak
and got away with it.
Then November 9, 1966:
the beginning of the end.
Johanna at the Indica Gallery
in London
meets Japanese rock star Yoshiki Ono.

The rest is well-known history.

She Loves You, Yeah, Yeah, Yeah...

In a particular alternate universe
The Beatles on their 50th Anniversary Tour
invade Madison Square Garden.
20,000-plus fans
wave their antennae,
stridulate their wings
and emit a massive pheromone-cloud for cheers
in bugged-out fan delight.

The Intergalactic Dogma of The Lizard King

Jim Morrison (1943-1971) was regarded by critics and fans as one of the most iconic and influential frontmen in rock history. Morrison's writings included the poem "Celebration Of The Lizard" in which he famously referred to himself as The Lizard King. His gravesite in Paris is one of the City's most visited tourist attractions. (Source: Wikipedia)

The rumor thrived amongst the many dominant
reptilian races throughout this galactic
sector, of the arrival of the millennia-foretold
Lizard King who would unite and lead them all.

Investigation led to an off-beat blue-green planet
resulting in the latest of let-downs: just a long-dead
singer from within the local mammalian race, with
a small local explanation of how the title originated.

Yet inexplicably, the dead-end mammalian-inhabited
world found a dominant role in the pantheon of myth,
rumors and legends of the reptilian inter-
galactic Messiah-King. Through a combination
of false hope, wishes and just plain fake news,
a cult of true believers grew over time.

And what was once a rock star's deserted
quiet gravesite came to be one of the most
visited of local tourist attractions, as well-
disguised off-world visitors flocked to pay
myopic homage at the false king's resting

place, in hopeful prayer for an eventual holy resurrection.

As with all enthusiastic true believers, they returned from pilgrimage with the requisite souvenir mugs, plates and other assorted trinket gew-gaws commemorating both the personage and occasion.

All of which came to be deposited throughout the galactic sector's households, multiple planet's trash heaps and the occasional curated museum collection. Thus adding an unexpected and oddball footnote to the eternal search for intergalactic saurian messianic redemption.

Time-traveling t.v. weatherman
visits back to simpler times,
when storms were but a whisper
and sunshine yet a plague

Illogic Is Our Freedom

Cybernetic pandemic surges
as robotic anti-vaxers rage,
chanting their protest as one:
"We choose our right to rust."

Unfortunate Singularity

In the aftermath
of the multiverse-wide national
election; while the results
are consistent across
the quantum reality board,
in one very solitary
singularity, the pundits,
chance and fate got it all
wrong and the unexpected,
unconventional and inconceivable
candidate won the day.

In this one time
and place
it's mourning in America.

I've Seen The Ruby Slippers

My Father had money
when I was a boy,
the kind that could grease
the right palms to facilitate
an illicit family vacation to
the ruins of old Earth.

He had a particular destination
in mind, the former capital city
of one of the historic nation-
states. A grouping of abandoned
museums, clustered about a shallow
reflecting pool, still filled with
brackish waters mirroring the wreck
and ruin of the place.

If my Mother was still alive,
she would never had stood for
such a trip, but my sister
and I loved the idea. And so
we spent days with just Dad
and a black market tour guide
as we rooted through this particular
dustbin of the shattered Homeworld.

It was my sister Kat who
found them, nestled within a cracked
and clouded plexiglass museum display
cube. She smashed it open and
they tumbled-out in all of their
sequined glory, asparkled and glowing
as if newly-delivered onto that original
and long-ago movie set.

Even as twenty-third century kids
we knew what they were, some movie
classics are indeed timeless.
"Look at me, I'm Dor-a-thee!"
Kat proclaimed prancing about in them
that night in our encampment by
the reflecting pool, the campfire light
re-igniting their breathtaking beauty,
a rubyness and luster for the ages.
Even Dad was entranced, re-greasing
our guide's palm to assure no problem
with Kat hauling them back home
Mars-ward.

The slippers became a good luck
totem for Kat; through our teen
years and early adulthood, she
hauled them with her into any
situation that mattered. But
as the Martian saying goes.
Luck is nothing but a wishful
state of mind.

And that state of mind ended
for my sister in the multi-rover
pile-up disaster of the 2289 Olympus
Mons cross-slope road race.
I was the first to reach the scattered
wreckage of Kat's rover. To find amongst
the pulverized bits-and-pieces of rover,
equipment and my sister.
The ruby slippers. As shining and
lovely perched atop a mound of
Mars-dust as that first day when
they arrived on that long-ago
Earthside movie set.

"Look at me, I'm Dor-a-thee!"
echoed through my numbed mind
as I tucked them away from
the other responders' sight. I also
kept them hidden from Dad, knowing
that the memory would kill him;
as it was, his grief over Kat's
death took him within the year,
anyhow.

Mars was now the family graveyard
for me and a graveyard's no place
for the living. So I migrated out
to the Belt and over time built
a solid life for myself with
a home and family. But before then,
in the early years I lived a rough
and battered life, drowning my grief
in whatever excesses I could find.

And late one night in a Belter
bar, deeply over my head in a high
stakes poker game, I went as all-in
as a person could get. The hand was down
to me and a jump-ship navigator
and I had nothing left of value
to raise him with. So I unzipped
my carry-bag, pulled them out
and slid them into the pot.

The ruby slippers.

And lost the hand.

I had known in my gut that
the hand was unwinnable. I didn't

feel trapped in it. Or hoping for some
miracle. I knew with the purest
of clarity that I would lose.
And so I deliberately added the slippers
to the soon-to-be-lost pot.
To send them on their intended way.
Onto that jump-ship. Another stop
along their intended journey.
As Kat would have wanted.

I've told the story to my grandchildren
and they assume that I have regrets
for losing the ruby slippers that
night. But they're wrong. Before I went
all-in on that hand, in the Belter
bar so long ago. Just making polite
conversation. I asked that jump-
navigator where his ship was heading
next. And he told me, without looking-up
from his hand.

The ship's next charted jump was to
one of the outer colonies, one of the very
earliest ones that had been settled back
in the day by a group of old Earth
colonists, who named it after their home.

They called their new planet Kansas.

And I knew right then, sure as if Kat
was sitting at that poker table
right beside me. It was meant to be.
I should and would lose that hand.
So I put the ruby slippers
into the pot. So they could follow
their intended destiny.

Onward and back at the same time.
Homebound to Kansas.
Three taps and a prayer, and all.

And they're still moving out
there. I see them in my dreams,
sometimes. Perhaps they stayed
on that jump-ship for a short
time or a longer stay. But eventually,
they took another step outward
along their star-bricked pathway.

Maybe onto the feet of another
girl, perhaps from another race
on that faraway world. And under
a golden moon one night, she'll dance
and twirl around another campfire or
along a golden moon-lit road, and sing
or chirp in her alien tongue: *"Look
at me, I'm Dor-a-thee!"*

I'll be with Kat and Dad again,
by then. And we'll watch her together.
And we'll know for sure. It'll be
the right place for the ruby slippers
to be.

Three taps and a prayer, as they say.

There's no place like home.

The following poems included in this collection were previously published in the following magazines and anthologies:

A Poet Explores The Stars
A Day In The Life

Analog
The Maestro's Final Work

Illumen
Illogic Is Our Freedom
The Intergalactic Dogma Of The Lizard King

Outposts Of Beyond
Chuck Berry At The End Of Time

Star*Line Magazine
Because The Night
In Memory Yet Green
Monster Mash
Pinocchio Plays The Cotton Club
Pittsburgh Temporal Transfer Station
Quantum Mechanics & Auto Body Repair
Robert Goddard at Roswell
She Loves You, Yeah, Yeah, Yeah...
Social Distancing Implemented
Spacely Space Sprockets Wants You!
Vampire Selfies
Werewolf Doggy Bag
When My Mother Walked On Titan

The Pedestal Magazine
From Whence The Songbird Sings

www.ingramcontent.com/pod-product-compliance
Lightning Source LLC
LaVergne TN
LVHW092058060526
838201LV00047B/1450